OLD HOUSE BASICS

BY
SCOTT SIDLER

WHO NEEDS THIS BOOK?

If you own or are renovating an older home (pre-1950s) this book is for you! Old homes are tricky. They're not complicated (actually they are quite simple to care for) they are just different from modern houses. They were made of different materials with different techniques than their modern day counterparts, and understanding those differences is the best way to save not only the intrinsic historical value of your home but also its financial value.

Remodels and improvements that would add value to a new house can unknowingly erode your old home's value. In this book, I've compiled a list of things every old house owner should know. I call them the "Old House Basics." Knowing these 20 basic pieces of information can save you from making some of the most typical mistakes homeowners make.

Learn your "Old House Basics" and you'll save yourself a whole heap of time, frustration, and money over the years. Remember, these are just the basics. There is a lot more to learn in order to protect your biggest investment.

These old houses are more valuable than you may think and in this book I'll show you where the value resides and how to save it and restore the things that really matter.

You'll learn some cool history and fun facts like, is glass a liquid or not? These old houses don't come with a manual, but hopefully this book with be the Quick-Start guide to owning an old house.

If you want to delve deeper, I'd suggest reading through the wealth of articles on my blog, or if you need help with a project, my company <u>Austin Historical</u> specializes in restoring historic windows and historic consulting all across America. We work day in and day out helping people just like you restore historic homes and buildings to shine like they once used to.

If you need help, don't hesitate to visit the blog at <u>TheCraftsmanBlog.com</u> or give us a call at (800) 611-2601. Now, on to the Old House Basics!

THE BASICS

#1 Wood Floors (Older is better)

The wood floors in homes built before the 1940s are made of some of the highest quality solid wood that was ever grown. Before the lumber industry cut down the old-growth forests that covered America, there were centuries old trees with wood that was not only beautiful, but also extremely durable and rot-resistant.

If your house was built in this time period, then removing or covering up a treasure like old growth wood is a very bad idea. Just because they are old, maybe a little dirty, scratched or dented doesn't mean they can't be restored to look and function beautifully once again.

Removing problem boards and replacing them with salvaged floor boards from the same era (maybe even stealing some from a closet) is a tried and true method or restoration that is easily done by a handy DIYer or local carpenter.

Years of paint and carpet glue or other unknown gunk can be quickly sanded off by a quality wood floor refinisher for between $2.50 and $4 a square foot which is easily much cheaper than the cost of materials and installation for any kind of new flooring.

They may look rough now, but don't give up on your old wood floors. They can and should be restored!

#2 Keep it Painted

If a list of to-do items were ranked by importance, to ensure your home remains in good working order over the years, proper painting would be at the top.

Keeping the outside of your home painted properly will keep water at bay and prevent rot. When your paint wears out, your home's elements are exposed to the weather, and the elements immediately start to ruin the structure and finish of your home.

Structures that were never painted to begin with and have no issues to speak of may be an exception because they have proven themselves, but if your house has already been painted, then keeping a consistent layer of paint across the exterior surfaces is imperative.

As paint wears and gets small holes, it provides a place for water to get in and get trapped and water is the biggest enemy of an old house.

Quality paint matters here too. Don't skimp when it comes to the cost of exterior paint. Paint is your home's shield and you want the best shield you can afford. Besides that, 90% of the cost of painting a house is the labor so why skimp on the last 10%? When it comes to paint, you truly get what you pay for so buy the best you can afford.

Moral of the story, if you want your home to last, keep it painted.

#3 DON'T GIVE UP ON YOUR WINDOWS

My greatest passion when it comes to old houses is to preserve their old windows. Whether they are wood or steel, original historic windows are not the energy-hogging, deathtraps the window replacement companies will tell you. They should be saved and here's why.

First, unlike new windows, they have lasted and can last for centuries with minimal maintenance. The windows of today are design to be disposable products you change out every 10-20 years. That's not how original windows were built.

They can be restored and repaired in part or in whole to look beautiful and function smoothly either by you or by a company like mine that specializes in historic window restoration.

Second, original windows are energy efficient. Not even counting the wastefulness of throwing dozens of old windows in the landfill and all the energy required to make and deliver new windows, these original windows have been tested by various groups and found to be more efficient than the current energy codes require.

All it takes is adding simple weatherstripping and an exterior or interior storm window and you can exceed the energy efficiency of a new double-paned replacement window. Plus, once restored, you can be assured they will last much longer than any replacement window which has a very finite lifespan before it fogs up and requires replacement...again.

Don't fall into the trap of replacing your windows when they can remain the beautiful, hand-crafted piece of your old house that they deserve to be.

#4 Plaster is a Good Thing

What's better plaster or drywall? Well, one is 1" thick and the other is only 1/2" thick. One is essentially made from limestone which is slowly curing and pulling carbon dioxide out of the environment while the other is paper covered gypsum.

Can you tell which I prefer? Of course it's plaster and that's for several reasons. Compared to drywall, plaster is thicker, stronger, better at sound proofing, and easier to repair in an unnoticeable way.

It's worth maintaining your historic plaster whether it's flat walls and ceilings or ornamental plaster moldings and medallions.

You may ask why plaster isn't used in construction anymore and the answer is simple, because it's just too expensive.

Plaster is a premium product that requires a skilled craftsman to apply, unlike drywall which is cheap to make, quick to install, and fits our standard one-size fits all mentality today.

You may not pay the extra expense to install plaster walls on a new house today, but if you already have it why would you get rid of it?

Yes, it may have dents, dings, and cracks but those can be patched if they really bother you. Even missing sections or sagging plaster that has come loose is fairly simple to repair if you know how.

When you have a premium product like plaster why would you replace it with something inferior like drywall? Keep the good stuff!

#5 Are Antique Fixtures Worth It?

You might be thinking that your antique fixtures are a fire hazard. Well, they might be, but it's nothing that can't be fixed by any lamp shop or with a quick trip to the hardware store.

Don't toss the old fixtures. Get them rewired and they will be as safe as a new fixture. Give them a cleaning and put them back into service.

Antique fixtures add so much value to an old home, especially if they are original. People pay a high price for restoration style hardware from replica companies like Rejuvenation or Restoration Hardware so if you've got it it's worth keeping.

The same goes for old plumbing fixtures. Plumbing technology hasn't changed much at all in the last hundred years. So while you may not be able to find a particular piece here or there, new seals and a new set screw may be all that stands between you and a vintage faucet that would be a true conversation piece of your home.

Vintage sinks and tubs may be rusting with chipped porcelain but by having them professionally reglazed for just a couple hundred dollars you can bring them back to life again and again rather than tossing them in the landfill and replacing them with a modern substitute that likely won't be the same quality.

#6 Linoleum is NOT Vinyl

Most people think that vinyl and linoleum flooring are the same. They are not. Vinyl is a modern product made from petroleum products.

Linoleum? It's made from all-natural products like canvas and linseed oil (hence the name Lin-oleum). Linoleum is naturally anti-microbial, continues to harden over the years, has color throughout its body, unlike vinyl which has a thin color layer on top and off-gasses potentially dangerous fumes for years.

Plus, linoleum has been around since the 1800's so it can be historically accurate. It's not always a cheap fix from the 60s or 70s that you might think it is. Historical linoleum is a great product if it's in good shape since it's soft under foot and warm in the winter compared to tile and it does great in high traffic or wet areas like kitchens.

Before you tear it out, know which one you have and think about what it might look like when cleaned and restored.

I understand that it may not be on your "keep" list, but knowing that it is an option is a good thing. That being said, I understand if you are trying to get back down to the original wood floors hiding underneath and won't lose too much sleep over it.

#7 The "No Maintenance" Paradox

It seems that everything today is no maintenance. You never have to clean it, never have to paint, never have to think about it ever again. If these products sound too good to be true, that's because they are.

If someone is trying to sell you a "no maintenance" home product an alarm as should go off in your head. Run the other direction, because "no maintenance" usually means it cannot be maintained. Many of these items do more damage than they do good.

A couple examples? Vinyl windows, vinyl siding, aluminum siding, PVC trim, and the list goes on and on.

If you can't maintain it, then you can't fix it. So when you call the manufacturer about a broken widget the typical response is "Oh, we don't make that piece anymore but we can sell you a new [item you need to fix]."

Even the toughest things in the world need occasional maintenance. Bricks, for example, last centuries but need repointing after a century or so. If it's repairable, then that means it can be renewed and repaired rather than thrown in the trash and a replacement purchased.

Only disposable products are maintenance free.

#8 Replace With Replicas

If you've got a broken doorknob or light switch, a cracked sash lock or cabinet pull, then the best option for an old house is to find a historic replica.

Van Dykes Restorers and House of Antique Hardware are good places to start shopping for replicas of old home parts along with a slew of smaller websites that specialize in salvage or restoration quality hardware and home parts.

Putting a new off-white light switch in a house with antique mother-of-pearl light switch buttons might work for a couple days to keep the lights on, but ultimately you should be looking for something that will match what you had and blend in with the quality of your old home's pieces.

When it comes to larger architectural items that have gone missing like original windows or moldings, my company Austin Historical can help you out there with a matching replica that only you will know is a replacement. Whether it's my company or someone else, matching the intricate details is important.

A historical replica helps to keep the style of the home consistent, and a consistent style is always good for value and continuity. Keep the historic nature of your historic house with a quality replica and you'll be glad in the end.

#9 Insulation Isn't That Important

Too many people tear out the old walls of their home and remove original moldings and features all in the name of adding insulation. Insulation is important, but there are ways you can insulate without tearing down the walls and ceilings.

Spend a little time investigating non-invasive methods on my blog and focus on areas with the greatest payback like attics and roofs.

Insulating your walls is way down the list of energy saving projects for an old house, despite what your insulation contractor may tell you. The majority of heat loss and gain from any house is through the "stack effect" which happens when warm air pours out of holes in the attic which creates a vacuum downstairs pulling in cold air from any opening it can.

Air sealing is the key! Weatherstripping windows and doors as well as sealing gaps at baseboards and around crawlspaces and in the attic slows down the air transfer. Then put a big blanket of insulation on your attic floor and you'll notice huge gains for very little money.

The mess of tearing out plaster walls and ripping off siding for a deep energy retrofit is a luxury that is expensive and rarely worthwhile unless you have money to burn. And if you have money to burn, I'll give you my address later.

#10 Wood Can Always Be Refinished

Even when it has been beat up beyond recognition, wood can almost always be refinished. I talked about floors earlier but this really applies to any woodwork in an old house.

Whether it's floors, balusters, baseboards, trim, or any number of wood items in your old home, chances are it can be stripped and refinished.

If it's going to be painted, you can repair huge sections of rot or termite damage using epoxies or other patching materials that can save you the added expense of buying replacements.

And if you have varnished woodwork, then dutchman patches can get you where you need to be for an attractive repair. We talked about "old-growth" earlier and it's not just on your floors but in your other woodwork too.

This custom woodwork that would likely be prohibitively expensive to build today may be expensive or time consuming if you plan to do it yourself to restore, but the end result is wood with beautiful character and rich color that is so worth the work.

Before you tear it out, do a little test section to see what's hiding behind all those decades of paint. You might be surprised to find something extraordinary hiding there!

#11 Salvage Yard Salvation

The architectural salvage yard is like the old home toy store. They have historic pieces for most anything you need to replace including: windows, doors, hardware, sinks, tubs, lights, siding, and so much more.

When you're in a pinch and can't find a replacement piece that would otherwise be very expensive to make, a salvage yard is a great place to search.

There aren't a ton of these stores around the country, but with the advent of the internet it doesn't really matter if there isn't one in your neck of the woods. Do a quick Google search and send some pictures along with measurements and it usually doesn't take long to find what you're looking for. You won't find mass quantities, but for a few select pieces you'll rarely strike out.

Not only can you find all this great stuff, but it is usually available at a huge discount. Sometimes you'll find fully restored pieces, but usually it will be old dirty items requiring you to put in the elbow grease to clean them up and put them back into service, and that's what gets you the great pricing on what would otherwise be extremely pricey items.

Gather the details and send them off to a few salvage yards before you spend the money on a replica or replacement.

#12 It's the Trees, Stupid

Siting a home and wisely incorporating landscaping in strategic areas is often overlooked today. But in the old days, homes were planned with deciduous trees planted on the south and west sides of the home to shield it from the hot summer sun. Then in the winter when the sun is lower in the horizon, those same trees had lost their leaves and allowed the winter sun into the house for much needed warmth.

This basic idea lasted centuries until we started building suburbs where we clear cut everything and planted a single scrawny tree at the curb.

For my taste, you can't beat the look of a century old oak sprawling over your house. If you're lucky enough to have this, then do everything you can to protect and maintain those trees.

If you don't have the trees that your old house deserves, I implore you to have the selflessness to plant and care for a shade tree that the next owner's children will get to enjoy. Maybe you'll live there long enough to enjoy the tree, but even if you don't, you can enjoy knowing that someone will appreciate your gesture. After all none of the towering trees around today were planted by anyone who is still around the enjoy them. Return the favor.

#13 Get the Lead Out

Lead paint was all too common in houses built before 1978 and can be a real danger, especially to children under six and to pregnant women. So, before you scrape, sand, or do anything to painted surfaces in your house make sure you protect yourself and your family.

The EPA has come up with extensive rules for remodeling older homes, and you need to be educated about them before you hire anyone to come in and work on your house. Either hire an EPA licensed professional to handle your project, or test for lead yourself and take the appropriate precautions.

Undisturbed lead paint that isn't peeling or chipping is not an acute danger. It's only when the lead becomes airborne or little children eat paint chips or chew on window sills that it becomes an issue. So, you don't need to have the lead abated unless it is in bad shape.

But every time you renovate an old house a ton of dust is created and it settles on everything. That is when the danger occurs and why the EPA has created the RRP work rules and licensing to make sure your contractor contains the dust and keeps you safe.

If your contractor is not RRP licensed, then they are skirting the law. Check their licensing and make sure you've got the right company.

#14 FORM FOLLOWS FUNCTION

Especially in much older homes, form follows function. The design of a particular item gets its shape and placement from the function it performs.

In old homes, there were rarely things like faux wood beams or fake shutters. Every element had a purpose and a function, even if you're not sure what it is. It's sometimes hard to put your finger on why a replacement element looks slightly off, and a lot of times it comes down to this principle.

Faux shutters, for example, are a big pet peeve of mine. As I like to say, "real shutters, shut" and if your shutter can't shut, you're already on shaky ground with me. Real shutters are exactly half the size of the window they are installed on otherwise they won't actually cover and protect the window like they were intended to. Most faux shutter are far too small, often built with the fake slats installed upside down and all other kinds of things that violate the form follows function principle.

It may not irk you on a conscious level like it does me, but there is a subconscious level of proper proportions and design that affects all of us and when we see something incorrect, it creates a level tension of and discomfort.

Before you change something, make sure you know what it is and just how important to your home it might be. You don't want to alter something that creates an awkwardness, or ruins a function you had no idea was important to the overall house.

#15 Asbestos, Asbestos, Asbestos

Hailed as the miracle of its time, asbestos can be found in scores of different building materials like vinyl floor tiles, insulation, roof tiles, siding shingles, plaster, window glazing putty, caulk, and more. It was everywhere and insurance companies used to give homeowners big discounts for installing it.

Until we knew the dangers of asbestos, we had figured out the massive benefits. It is rot proof, fireproof, insect proof, naturally occurring, plentiful, and cheap. It was added to all kinds of things to help them last longer and perform better. Sadly, it poses a major health risk when it is cut sanded crushed or otherwise modified so that the fibers become airborne.

Similarly to lead paint, if you have asbestos that is in good shape and isn't being disturbed, then it doesn't require abatement unless you want to. When it is in poor shape like crumbling pipe insulation or chipping shingles, or it's in an area that plans to be remodeled, that is when the danger comes.

Before you disturb any questionable area, send a small sample to a testing facility just to be sure this dangerous material isn't involved. If it is, you should be calling a specially trained and licensed asbestos abatement company to remove the materials and declare it safe for the renovation to begin. You can't be too careful!

#16 Old Brick are Softies

If your brickwork needs repair, you should be careful to use bricks and mortar from the same time period as the existing brickwork. Not only does a repair that doesn't match the original brickwork look terrible, but old bricks and mortar are softer than modern bricks and modern mortar.

Intermixing generations can cause your old bricks to self-destruct by falling victim to something called spalling. Spalling occurs when the mortar is harder than the brick and through seasonal expansion and contraction, the hard mortar eventually crushes the face of the brick turning it into powder.

Another issue with modern mortar is that it does not allow moisture migration at the same rates as historic limes mortars. That isn't a problem if you have a new building, but when you have old bricks and new mortar, the moisture is forced through the brick face rather than being expelled through the mortar face, which results in an ugly condition called efflorescence which is when salts are deposited on the brick face.

Moral of the story, find a mason who specializes in historic buildings before you have any work done.

#17 Wavy Glass is Good Glass

That old wavy glass in your windows can be annoying if you're not used to it. But once you come to appreciate the uniqueness, of it I bet you'll think differently.

Believe it or not, that glass is worth more than the new stuff. The new stuff is just too perfect for some of us who long for the character of hand-blown glass windows. And wavy glass, or "glimmer glass" as it is sometimes called, is quickly disappearing from old homes as it breaks or is thrown out.

Wavy glass was manufactured by either hand-blowing or machine-blowing glass and then spinning or swinging the glass to stretch it out into discs or tubes depending on the age of the glass. This resulted in the irregular appearance since centrifugal force affected the glass irregularly.

Contrary to popular myth, glass is not a liquid and isn't flowing downward on your old windows. Because of the manufacturing process, the glass was not all a uniform thickness and the glazier who made your windows, as a matter of practice, would install the thicker side of the pane at the bottom for a more stable window and to prevent undue stress on the thinnest part of the glass.

Learn to appreciate the waves and bubbles as character and you'll enjoy the view from your 100% unique windows since no glass is the same. There's no reason to replace it, save for a stray baseball that is.

#18 CALL A SPECIALIST

Your old home needs a specialist not just a general contractor. If you are having work done, make sure anyone you hire understands and is sensitive to working with the unique materials in your old home.

I've seen too many historic homes have their value destroyed by well intentioned but clueless contractors who had no idea how to work on an old home.

I've already listed so many things that are different about old houses, but the list is even more extensive than what I can cover here. The point is, you need someone who understand this list intimately.

Just like you take your children to a pediatrician because they have studied in depth about how children's bodies work and what they need to grow into healthy adults, a historical specialist knows the details of what your old house needs better than anyone else.

This is a service my company offers nationwide because there just seems to be a lack of historical specialists compared to the number of historic properties that need them. Find someone you can trust locally or give us a call and we'll walk you through the details of your project so that you can check all the boxes and get it done right.

This is especially true if you are renovating a project for a tax credit or grant program where they have specific processes you have to follow in order to get your funding. Guessing on the right way to renovate and old building can cost big money in mistakes that didn't need to be made.

#19 Little Stuff Isn't so Little

All the innumerable details of your old home like light switches, door knobs, window hardware, moldings, trim, lights, plumbing fixtures, etc., add up to define the character of your home.

I've talked about picking replicas when something is missing or searching salvage yards and restoring old pieces when possible, but this applies to things that may not seem like a big deal.

Window and door hardware is often beautifully ornate solid bronze items that you'd never know were important or beautiful because they are caked with so much paint. It may take a little detective work to see what you have hiding, but more often than not I am pleasantly surprised by what I find.

Replace these unique items with generic home store stuff and you strip your home of its identity and value. Some may need repair or restoration, but if paint removal is the biggest hurdle you face, it's worth a second thought before you replace it.

My suggestion would be to move slowly before replacing anything you're not absolutely sure what it is or what its condition is.

#20 It's Not Good Because It's Old, It's Old Because It's Good

This pretty much sums up the whole old home experience in my mind. Some people will think it's weird to save and restore all the pieces, big and small, that go into an old home, but the reason these pieces of your home have survived so long is because they are quality products made in a time when it was more important to make something right than to make it fast.

Don't get confused that you should save these parts because they are old. You should save them because they are good! The reason these old houses have stood the test of time and deserve to be preserved is because these are the best of the best. They have made it through decades of brutal weather, awful handymen, and careless renters.

They are the last remaining connection to a time and a people that have passed into the history book. Still, they stand here as a memory of a different time and a different way of building things when we cared a little more about leaving something for those that came after us.

The poorly built houses from centuries past have all fallen prey to time and mother nature and been forgotten, but your house is still here and it's up to you to keep it so that the next generation can experience the only link to the past that they can still touch and interact with in a way a book won't allow.

Going Further

If you've enjoyed this book and you want to learn more about old homes or need help on an upcoming project, I'd love to hear from you! You can always visit my blog to learn more at TheCraftsmanBlog.com or email me at Info@AustinHistorical.com. I'd also love to connect with you on our social media pages below.

- Facebook @AustinHistorical
- Instagram @AustinHistorical and @TheCraftsmanBlog
- YouTube @TheCraftsmanBlog

Old home owners need to stick together because we're a special breed of people willing to put up with and take care of these old buildings.

The biggest danger to most old houses is a lack of knowledge as to what's important and what the old school techniques to restore them are. That's why I wrote this book; to share what I've learned from years as a preservation contractor so you can be better prepared. Good luck!

If you need help with your historic building my company Austin Historical restores historic wood and steel windows and offers historical consulting for projects all across the country. We'd love to hear about your restoration project at (800) 611-2601 or Info@AustinHistorical.com.

Printed in the USA
CPSIA information can be obtained
at www.ICGtesting.com
LVHW050502260724
786473LV00002BA/219